WORKING TOWARD ABOLISHING SLAVERY

Tim Cooke

CRABTREE
PUBLISHING COMPANY
WWW.CRABTREEBOOKS.COM

CRABTREE
PUBLISHING COMPANY
WWW.CRABTREEBOOKS.COM

Author: Tim Cooke
Picture Manager: Sophie Mortimer
Designer: Lynne Lennon
Design Manager: Keith Davis
Children's Publisher: Anne O'Daly
Editorial director: Kathy Middleton
Editor: Janine Deschenes
Proofreader: Wendy Scavuzzo
Print coordinator: Katherine Berti

Photographs: (t=top, b= bottom, l=left, r=right, c=center)

Front Cover: Alamy: Charles Edwards (bottom center), Chronicle (center left); Shutterstock: John Gomez (bottom left and center right)

Interior: Alamy: Stephen Chung 41, Everett Collection 18; Library of Congress: 26, 27; National Portrait Gallery: 20; Public Domain: 24, Afro-American Press 21b. Art Catalog Russia 32, Bair175 35, CEE-HOPe NIGERIA 34, Delaware Art Museum 17, Devonish 33, General Archives of the Indies 9, Magharebia 38, New Haven Colony Historical Society 19; Shutterstock: 39, 1000 words 7, Elton Abreu 31, Amani A 40, Arindam Banerjee 10, Gerard Botting 43, CasimoPT 37, John Gomez 1, 5b, Everett Collection 4, 5t, 6–7, 11, 12, 13, 14, 15, 16, 21t, 22, 23, 25, 28, 29, Danny Fabian 8, Alexandros Michalidis 36, Dr Morley Read 30, Debbie Ann Powell 15, 44.

Brown Bear Books has made every attempt to contact the copyright holder. If you have any information about omissions, please contact licensing@brownbearbooks.co.uk

Library and Archives Canada Cataloging in Publication

Title: Working toward abolishing slavery / Tim Cooke.
Names: Cooke, Tim, 1961- author.
Description: Series statement: Achieving social change | Includes bibliographical references and index.
Identifiers: Canadiana (print) 20200299441 | Canadiana (ebook) 20200299468 | ISBN 9780778779483 (softcover) | ISBN 9780778779421 (hardcover) | ISBN 9781427125460 (HTML)
Subjects: LCSH: Antislavery movements—Juvenile literature. | LCSH: Slavery—Juvenile literature. | LCSH: Abolitionists—Juvenile literature. | LCSH: African American abolitionists—Juvenile literature.
Classification: LCC HT1031 .C66 2021 | DDC j326/.8—dc23

Library of Congress Cataloging-in-Publication Data

Names: Cooke, Tim, 1961- author.
Title: Working toward abolishing slavery / Tim Cooke.
Description: New York : Crabtree Publishing Company, 2021. | Series: Achieving social change | Includes bibliographical references and index.
Identifiers: LCCN 2020032442 (print) | LCCN 2020032443 (ebook) | ISBN 9780778779421 (hardcover) | ISBN 9780778779483 (paperback) | ISBN 9781427125460 (ebook)
Subjects: LCSH: Antislavery movements--Juvenile literature. | Slavery--Juvenile literature. | Abolitionists--Juvenile literature. | African American abolitionists--Juvenile literature.
Classification: LCC HT1031 .C66 2021 (print) | LCC HT1031 (ebook) | DDC

Crabtree Publishing Company
www.crabtreebooks.com **1-800-387-7650**

Published in Canada
Crabtree Publishing
616 Welland Ave.
St. Catharines, ON
L2M 5V6

Published in the United States
Crabtree Publishing
347 Fifth Ave
Suite 1402-145
New York, NY 10016

Published by CRABTREE PUBLISHING COMPANY in 2021

Printed in the U.S.A./092020/CG20200810

CONTENTS

INTRODUCTION

Slavery is the ownership of one person by another. People often associate it with the enslavement of Black Africans in North America. In fact, it existed in many forms in the past—and still exists today.

For as long as slavery has existed, people have objected to it. Today, it is widely believed that it is wrong for one human to be able to own another like an object, or to control another person against his or her will.

Children of an enslaved person also became the property of his or her owner, so whole generations lived in slavery.

Forms of Resistance

Resistance to slavery took many forms. Enslaved people staged individual acts of **rebellion**, such as failing to obey orders or breaking their owners' possessions. Others tried to escape or to remove their owners from power. Some enslaved people who escaped became leaders calling for the **abolition** of slavery.

These leaders described the miseries of life as an enslaved person. Their evidence made it more difficult for people to ignore the realities of slavery.

Other types of resistance came from campaigns that pressured governments to outlaw slavery. In the 1900s, religious groups, charities, and organizations such as the United Nations introduced measures to make slavery illegal.

Activists against slavery included former enslaved people such as Frederick Douglass, who told their stories and urged others to take action.

A Continuing Problem

Today, slavery survives in different forms in parts of the world. It is still the target of **reform** movements. As in the past, activists against slavery include former enslaved people. Other campaigns are part of the activities of organizations that work to support **human rights** for everyone.

*Campaigns against modern slavery target **human trafficking**, in which people are forced to work against their will.*

CHAPTER 1

WHAT IS SLAVERY?

The best-known form of slavery is probably that of Black Africans in the Americas from the 1600s to the 1800s. There have been many other forms, however. Some have other names, but they are all types of slavery.

Enslaved Africans in North America were bought and sold like goods. This is known as **chattel** slavery. Enslaved Africans had no legal rights. They and their children became the property of their owners.

In South America, Spanish invaders forced **Indigenous** peoples to work on ranches or in mines. This is called forced labor. In this type of enslavement, someone is put to work against his or her will, usually by the threat of punishment. However, the person is not owned by anyone else, and has some legal rights. Forced labor still goes on. Poor people are often made to work in industries such as agriculture, or farming.

This illustration shows a woman being sold into slavery at an auction in the United States in 1856. A Black trader looks on. There were a small number of Black owners who had been able to buy their way out of slavery.

Poor workers around the world are forced or tricked into working with no means of quitting or finding a new job.

Bonded Labor

Other forms of slavery include **indentured** labor and **bonded** labor. Both involve people being forced to work to pay off a debt. Some terms of bonded labor, however, trick people into working for an unlimited time.

Women and children are often particularly at risk of being forced into slavery. Women and girls end up in forced marriages without their **consent**. These marriages can include forced labor or trafficking. In child slavery, children are forced to work to make money for someone else.

Other forms of modern slavery are linked with criminal activity such as human trafficking. People trying to escape poverty are illegally forced to work, either in their own country or a different country.

Slavery in History

Slavery is an ancient practice. As the nature of slavery has changed over time, so has the nature of the objections against it.

Ancient societies, such as the Greeks and Romans, had large numbers of enslaved people. Some enslaved people held respected roles, such as running their owner's household or business. Enslaved people sometimes had the right to own property themselves, and many were freed. Still, a few people objected to slavery. The Greek philosopher Alcidamas claimed, "No one is made a slave by nature." Although the early Christian church called for enslaved people to be freed, it did not call for the end of slavery itself.

Enslaved women help their owner in ancient Rome. Even at the time, some people called slavery "unnatural."

Fighting Against Slavery

The transatlantic slave trade, which brought enslaved Africans across the Atlantic Ocean, began in the early 1500s. More than 12.5 million Africans were brought to the Caribbean, Brazil, and North America. By 1860, the United States had 4 million enslaved people.

In 1537, after protests from Catholic **missionaries**, the Pope made the enslavement of local peoples illegal, or not allowed by law, in South America. From the mid-1600s, Christian groups such as **Quakers** spoke against slavery in North America. Other activists were formerly enslaved people. In Europe, formerly enslaved people joined activists who tried to convince governments to make slavery illegal in their **empires**.

In the 1900s, the campaign against slavery was increasingly taken up by organizations such as the National Association for the Advancement of Colored People (NAACP), which included many Black Americans. International organizations also campaigned against slavery. They included the United Nations, which was formed in 1945.

The Spanish priest Bartolomé de las Casas spoke out against the enslavement of Native peoples in Spanish ***colonies*** *such as Mexico.*

Viewpoints

There have been supporters and opponents of slavery throughout much of history. That situation continues today. Supporters of modern slavery often claim that it is simply a form of employment practice.

Arguments against slavery are usually based on **moral** grounds. Most people believe that it is wrong to treat a human being in the same way as an animal or even a piece of furniture. It is also wrong to deprive people of rights, such as the right to decide how they live and the right to earn money from their labor. In the past, people also objected that slavery would eventually lead to unrest.

This family in India is under forced labor to make bricks. Around the world, people are ***exploited*** *in conditions similar to slavery.*

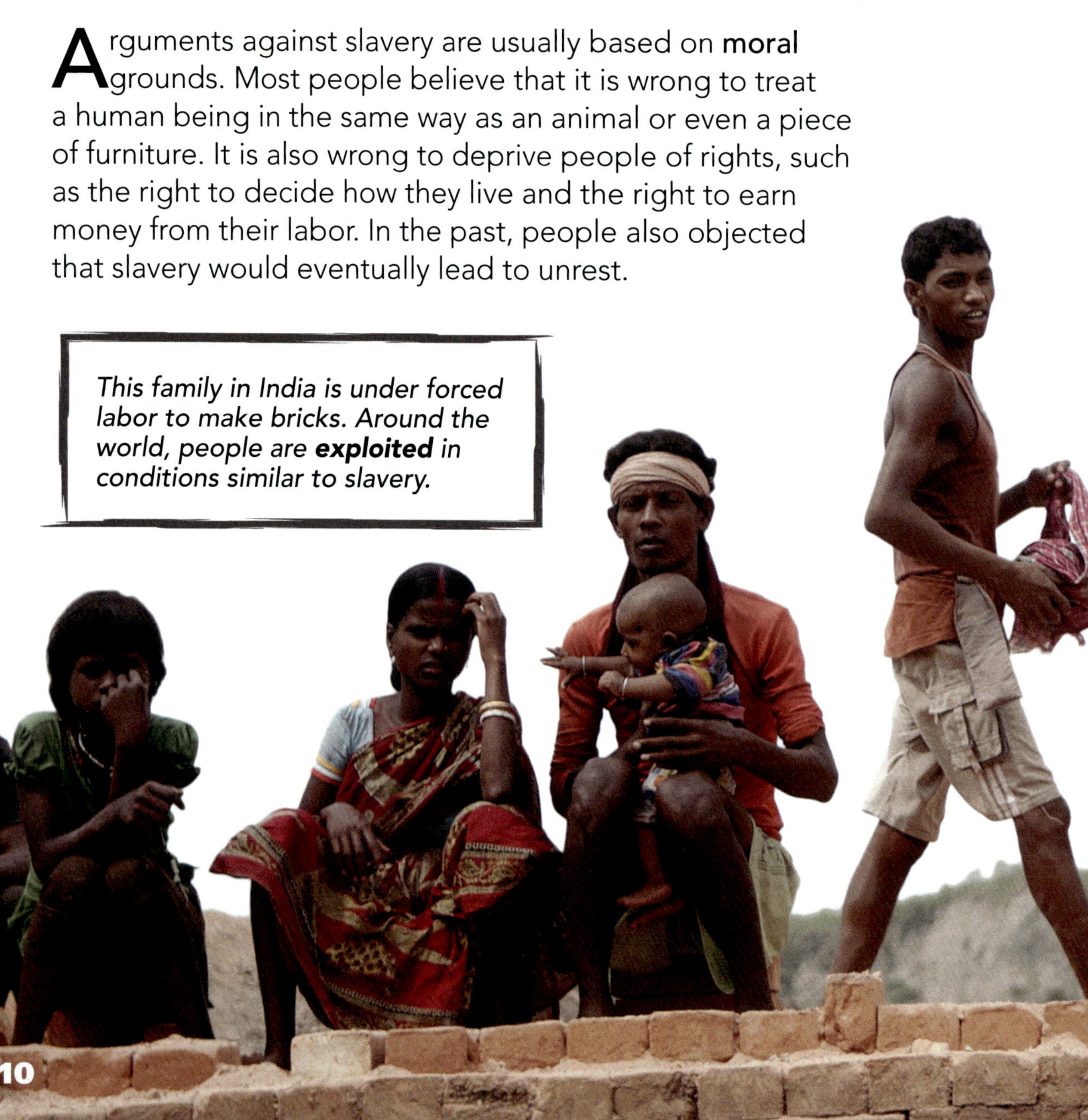

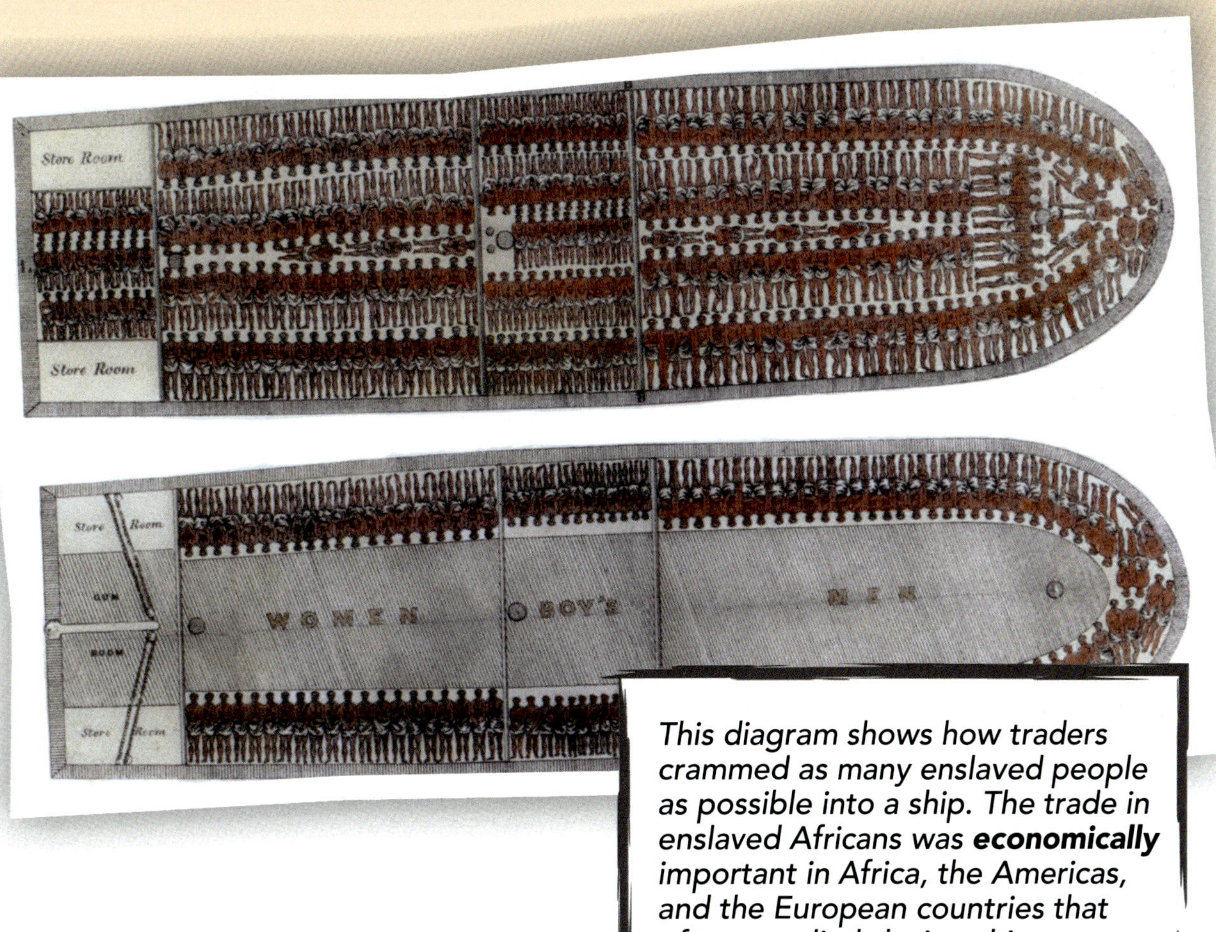

This diagram shows how traders crammed as many enslaved people as possible into a ship. The trade in enslaved Africans was ***economically*** *important in Africa, the Americas, and the European countries that often supplied slaving ships.*

A Normal State

In the past, some claimed that slavery was a normal part of life. Slavery based on race was justified by the incorrect idea that the enslaved group was inferior, or less intelligent and capable, than others. In the 1800s, for example, owners of enslaved people in the American South wrongly claimed to offer enslaved people a better life than they would have in "**barbarian**" Africa.

Most often, the justification for slavery has been economic. The agricultural economy of the Caribbean or the American South in the 1800s would have failed without free labor. That convinced many people to accept the existence of slavery. In the same way, consumers today might buy cheap clothes made in Asia, even though they know the work may be done by people who are paid little or are forced to work.

CHAPTER 2

EARLY RESISTANCE

Jean-Baptiste Sans-Souci looked over the battlefield in the mountains of northern Saint-Domingue—later called Haiti. It was covered with the bodies of French soldiers. The formerly enslaved person had become a fierce military leader.

Born in central Africa, Sans-Souci was enslaved and shipped to the French colony of Saint-Domingue. There, he joined a **revolt** against slavery. In 1795, the rebels won control. Led by Toussaint Louverture, who had been born into slavery, they set up a government and abolished slavery. In 1802, the French fought back. Some of the rebels joined the French briefly before rejoining the Saint-Domingue forces.

French soldiers arrive in Saint-Domingue in 1802 to try to take back control of the island from the government set up by formerly enslaved people.

> I was born a slave, but nature gave me the soul of a free man.
>
> Toussaint Louverture

Toussaint Louverture was born into slavery. He was a leader of the revolution before he gradually extended his control over Saint-Domingue. He became Saint-Domingue's governor-general in 1796.

Sans-Souci refused to work with anyone who had switched sides in this way. His refusal angered other leaders in Saint-Domingue, who had Sans-Souci killed in 1803. The following year, Saint-Domingue became fully independent from France and was renamed Haiti. The revolution in Haiti was the first successful rebellion by enslaved people.

Equality for Some

In 1789, the French had started a revolution, claiming that all men were equal. When free Blacks in Saint-Domingue claimed the right to vote, the French revolutionaries disagreed. This failure to recognize the rights of formerly enslaved people became one of the main triggers of the revolution in Haiti.

Escaping Slavery

Saint-Domingue was not the only place where enslaved peoples used armed resistance to try to achieve freedom. Other enslaved people also managed to form free communities.

Spanish colonists first brought enslaved people to Jamaica. When British forces invaded in 1655, many enslaved people escaped into the island's mountains. They formed communities with Indigenous peoples there, and other enslaved people joined them. Members of these communities became known as Maroons. The communities survived two conflicts with the British in the 1700s, called the Maroon Wars. Their descendants still live in parts of Jamaica.

*Maroon villages survived by farming and by raiding larger **plantations** on the island. These raids were also carried out to free enslaved people who worked on the plantations.*

North America

In British North America in the 1700s, many enslaved people escaped to Spanish Florida. They joined the Seminole, a Native American people, and lived freely. After Florida was taken over by the British in 1763, many headed north toward states in which slavery was illegal, or to Canada.

In the American Revolution (1775–1783), about 20,000 "Black **Loyalists**" fought with the British. They believed they had more chance of freedom under British rule. One of the Black Loyalists leaders, Colonel Tye, became famous for leading a military unit of formerly enslaved people who had escaped from Virginia.

Queen Nanny was the leader of a Maroon settlement called Nanny Town. She led military resistance against the British.

Key Voices

Leading Maroon Resistance

In the First Maroon War (1728–1739), British Redcoats, or troops, faced a fearsome enemy. Queen Nanny, or Nanny of the Maroons, had been born in Africa. She was enslaved and taken to Jamaica, where she joined the Maroons. She was skilled at certain war **tactics**, such as making surprise attacks on British troops. Her tactics were so effective that people said she was helped by supernatural forces.

Religious Objections

Some of the voices objecting to slavery came from religious groups. Many believed that only God could govern or control people, not other individuals.

Among them were people from Quaker and **Mennonite** communities. In 1688, Quakers in Pennsylvania wrote a *Petition Against Slavery*, which condemned the slave trade. In the 1730s and 1740s, Methodist and Baptist preachers spoke out against slavery. The campaign led to Pennsylvania banning slavery in 1780.

The Society for Effecting the Abolition of the Slave Trade was set up by Quakers in London. Its design showing an African man was widely reproduced in Britain and North America.

OBSERVATIONS

On the Inslaving, importing and purchasing of

Negroes;

With some Advice thereon, extracted from the Epistle of the Yearly-Meeting of the People called QUAKERS, held at *London* in the Year 1748.

When ye spread forth your Hands, I will hide mine Eyes from you, yea when ye make many Prayers I will not hear; your Hands are full of Blood. Wash ye, make you clean, put away the Evil of your Doings from before mine Eyes Isai. 1, 15.

Is not this the Fast that I have chosen, to loose the Bands of Wickedness, to undo the heavy Burden, to let the Oppressed go free, and that ye break every Yoke, Chap. 58, 7.

Second Edition.

GERMANTOWN:
Printed by CHRISTOPHER SOWER. 1760.

Key Voices

An Anti-Slavery Movement

French-born Anthony Benezet moved to America in 1731, having become a Quaker. Benezet argued that slavery did not fit with Quaker beliefs. He started the first anti-slavery movement in 1775, the Society for the Relief of Free Negroes Unlawfully Held in Bondage. It was renamed the Pennsylvania Abolition Society (PAS).

Absalom Jones's Free African Society included many former enslaved people freed after the American Revolution.

Questions of Inferiority

After the American Revolution, the Pennsylvania Society for Promoting the Abolition of Slavery or more simply the Pennsylvania Abolition Society (PAS) led by Anthony Benezet unsuccessfully tried to have slavery banned by the new U.S. Constitution in 1787. Although its 82 members wanted enslaved people to be freed, many also wrongly believed that Black Africans were inferior human beings.

In 1787, one of the first organizations for Black Americans began in Philadelphia. Absalom Jones and Richard Allen were both free Black clergymen born into slavery. They formed the Free African Society (FAS) to combat the idea that Africans were inferior to White people. Their argument questioned popular beliefs. It also challenged one of the core defenses that supporters of slavery used to justify its existence.

CHAPTER 3

MAKING PROGRESS

Joseph Cinqué had been enslaved in Africa and taken across the Atlantic Ocean to Cuba. There, he and around 50 others were bought by two Spaniards and taken onboard the *Amistad*. Cinqué decided to seize the ship.

The *Amistad* set sail for another part of Cuba, but on July 2, 1839, Cinqué persuaded the other enslaved men to act together. They overthrew the crew, killing the captain and the cook. Cinqué demanded that the Spanish crew members help the men sail to Africa. In fact, the Spaniards tricked the Africans into sailing toward the United States. There, the vessel was taken into harbor. The Africans were imprisoned for murder.

The events of the rebellion and the trial that followed were covered in newspapers in the United States and elsewhere.

> I am resolved that it is better to die than be a white man's slave.
>
> Joseph Cinqué

Joseph Cinqué and the other Africans returned home after the Supreme Court ruled that they were not enslaved people.

Making a Legal Case

The Spaniards claimed ownership of the Africans. They wanted to take them back to Cuba. The Africans argued that their enslavement was illegal, because the slave trade was forbidden in Cuba, even though slavery was legal there. The U.S. Supreme Court ruled in the Africans' favor. The case opened a new tactic. Activists could use legal arguments to free enslaved individuals, even if they could not make slavery itself illegal.

Elsewhere in the world, attitudes about slavery were changing. In Britain and France, for example, campaigners had convinced their governments to abolish slavery not just at home but also throughout their huge empires. This included countries such as Canada, India, and Australia, and large regions of North Africa and Southeast Asia.

A Growing Voice

The changing attitudes toward slavery were supported by a new type of activism. In 1791, a book entitled *The Interesting Narrative of the Life of Olaudah Equiano; or, Gustavus Vassa, the African, Written by Himself* told the story of a former enslaved person in his own words.

Equiano was kidnapped in Africa aged about 11 and enslaved in the Caribbean, Virginia, and Georgia. In 1766, his owner offered to sell him his freedom. Equiano accepted and moved to England. In 1781, he protested a case in which British slave traders threw 130 enslaved people overboard to claim **insurance** payments on their lives. The courts ruled that the killings were legal on the grounds that the ship had low supplies of fresh water. By speaking out against this, Equiano became well known.

Abolitionists asked Equiano to write about his own childhood in slavery. His book also described how he studied the Bible and went into business.

Equiano described the conditions faced by enslaved people working in the fields, as well as his own more fortunate position working in his owner's house.

A Shocking Insight

This was the first time most people had heard about experiences of a former enslaved person. Equiano's story went against the common argument by supporters of slavery that the experiences of enslaved people were generally positive. Equiano's book was followed by many other narratives throughout the 1800s. Writers such as Frederick Douglass, Harriet Jacobs, and Sojourner Truth told their stories as part of the campaign to reveal the truth about slavery.

Sojourner Truth escaped from slavery as a young mother and became a leading speaker in the cause for ending slavery.

FREEDOM'S JOURNAL.

"RIGHTEOUSNESS EXALTETH A NATION"

NEW-YORK, FRIDAY, MARCH 30, 1827.

Key Events

Anti-Slavery Newspapers

The written word was a powerful weapon against slavery. In 1827, a group of free Black men started an anti-slavery newspaper, *Freedom's Journal*, while *The Provincial Freeman* was founded in Canada in 1853. Most owners did not allow enslaved people to read for fear that ideas of rebellion would spread.

Violent Revolts

Some enslaved people tried using violence to escape from their owners. They were rarely successful. However, the rebels believed they had no other chance of achieving freedom.

Despite the success of the rebellion in Saint-Domingue, most uprisings of enslaved people ended in failure and punishment. In one of the first, in 1712, enslaved Africans burned a building in New York City. The authorities punished most of the suspects by death. After a revolt in South Carolina in 1739, about 20 armed enslaved people headed for Spanish Florida, where slavery was illegal. They were defeated by the South Carolina **militia**.

Enslaved people revolt on a sugar plantation in British Guiana (now Guyana) in 1823. More than 10,000 enslaved people took part, but were suppressed by British troops.

Defeated by Force

In the largest revolt, up to 500 enslaved people marched from the German Coast on the Mississippi River toward New Orleans in 1811. After two days, they were again defeated by the militia.

Two of the most violent uprisings were led by Denmark Vesey in South Carolina in 1822 and Nat Turner in Virginia in 1831. Turner often read the Bible. He believed God wanted him to free enslaved people. He and his followers killed up to 65 colonists as they freed enslaved people. The revolt was crushed by authorities. New laws forbade teaching enslaved people to read, so that they could not read the Bible as Turner had done.

Nat Turner (on the left) hid for six weeks before he was eventually captured. Along with about 50 others, he was tried and sentenced to death by hanging. The judges involved were owners of enslaved people.

Key Events

The Malê Revolt, Brazil

In January 1835, hundreds of enslaved people revolted in Brazil. Mostly African Muslims, called Malê, they observed **Islamic** practices in Brazil. The rebels were defeated, but the revolt made many Brazilians fear more uprisings. It began a process that led to the banning of the slave trade in Brazil in 1851, although slavery continued until 1888.

CHAPTER 4

TOWARD ABOLITION

In September 1849, Harriet Tubman crossed the border between Delaware and Pennsylvania. She had walked nearly 90 miles (150 km) from the plantation in Maryland were she had been born. She was free.

Something was missing at her new home, however. Harriet had to travel alone and leave her family behind. They were still enslaved in Maryland. Harriet later took on the difficult and dangerous task of going back there, first to free her sister's family and again to get her brothers. Seven years later, Harriet helped her parents escape to New York. In total, Harriet led many people to freedom and instructed many more how to escape by themselves.

> "I was free, but there was no one to welcome me to the land of freedom."
>
> Harriet Tubman

Harriet Tubman risked her life to lead hundreds of enslaved people, including her own family, to freedom.

A woman escaping from slavery is helped out of a small boat. Many Black and White Americans helped fugitives on the Underground Railroad.

The Underground Railroad

Harriet Tubman is best known for her work on the Underground Railroad. This was a secret network that helped enslaved people reach safety in the North and Canada, where slavery was illegal. As a "conductor," Harriet guided people on the dangerous journey to freedom. She became known as "Moses," after the prophet in the Bible who led his people to freedom from slavery. She discussed ways to end slavery with well-known abolitionists, including John Brown and Frederick Douglass. During the Civil War (1861–1865), Harriet joined the Union Army as a spy and a nurse. She led a military expedition that freed 750 enslaved people from South Carolina.

The Abolition Movement

The Underground Railroad was part of a number of campaigns and campaigners organized into what is known as the Abolition Movement. Those involved in the movement, known as abolitionists, called for the complete ending of slavery.

One of the most prominent abolitionists was Frederick Douglass. Douglass was enslaved in Maryland until he escaped in 1838 by disguising himself as a sailor and traveling by train to New York City. Describing his life as a free man, Douglass later said, "I lived more in one day than in a year of my slave life." Douglass moved to New Bedford, Massachusetts, where he became a preacher.

Douglass was inspired by White abolitionist William Lloyd Garrison, who published his ideas in a newspaper called The Liberator.

Key Events

Uncle Tom's Cabin is Published

In 1852, Harriet Beecher Stowe published *Uncle Tom's Cabin*. It was inspired by her horror at the 1850 Fugitive Slave Act, which stated that escaped enslaved people had to be sent back to slavery—even if they were caught in a free state. The novel described the suffering of an enslaved man named Tom. It suggested that Christian love could defeat the evils of slavery. The message was so powerful that the book sold 300,000 copies in the United States in its first year.

Douglass also began to attend abolitionist meetings and was invited to describe his own experiences. He was a commanding speaker, known for his powerful language that opened his audience's eyes to the cruelty of slavery.

Many Acts of Resistance

Speeches were one way that abolitionists showed resistance to slavery. Publications such as books and newspapers were another. Many abolitionists also carried out rescues of enslaved people. These important acts of resistance could result in activists being arrested and punished.

In 1858, prominent abolitionist Charles Henry Langston took part in the Oberlin-Wellington Rescue. When an escaped enslaved man was arrested by a U.S. marshall in Oberlin, Ohio, and taken to nearby Wellington, Langston joined other citizens to rescue him. They stormed the hotel where he was being held and hid him safely in Oberlin. Langston later arranged for the man's passage to freedom in Canada.

The Oberlin rescuers (above) were tried for their actions and eventually released. Langston was sentenced to 20 days in jail and a fine of $100. Later, abolitionists protested his sentencing.

Taking up Arms

In 1857, the U.S. Supreme Court ruled on a case brought by an enslaved man named Dred Scott. He and his wife had tried to claim their freedom because they had spent many years living in states where slavery was illegal.

The court ruled that enslaved people were not citizens, so could not bring legal cases. The judgment seemed to close all legal ways to end slavery. Anti-slavery campaigners were horrified. They included John Brown, who had already led violent attacks on pro-slavery settlements in the South. They tried to make people too frightened to own enslaved people. Now Brown plotted to raid the state **arsenal** at Harpers Ferry, Virginia, to seize arms to begin an uprising by enslaved people.

Dred Scott and his wife were freed by their owner a few months after the court case, but Scott died only a year later.

Key Voices

The Wilberforce Colony

John Brown sought support for his raid from settlements set up by Black Americans in Ontario, Canada. The Wilberforce Colony, for example, was founded in 1829 by free Blacks from Ohio. In Canada, they had legal rights they lacked in the United States. About 200 families eventually lived in the Wilberforce Colony, including escaped enslaved people who reached Canada.

Controversial Figure

Brown and 18 supporters seized the arsenal on October 16, 1859. The next day, U.S. Marines cornered them, killing 10 and capturing seven, including Brown. He was found guilty of treason and was hanged on December 2. He became a **martyr** for the anti-slavery cause, although people such as Frederick Douglass disagreed with his violent tactics.

The raid increased divisions in American society before the 1860 presidential election. The Republican candidate, Abraham Lincoln, was a critic of slavery. Southern states feared he would ban slavery, so they broke away from the Union. The Civil War began when Lincoln tried to prevent them from leaving. In 1863, Lincoln made the Emancipation Proclamation, declaring that enslaved people in the South would be freed. When the war ended in Union victory in 1865, all enslaved people in the United States were freed.

CHAPTER 5

CONTINUING STRUGGLES

Omarino had never seen anything like London. It was 1911, and the young man had been brought to the British capital from his home in the rain forests of the Amazon, where his people, the Witoto, were enslaved.

A **diplomat** named Roger Casement had brought Omarino and a friend, Ricudo, to London to expose enslavement of the Witoto by a British rubber company. The demand for rubber boomed in the late 1800s. The Peruvian Amazon Company enslaved at least 30,000 Witoto and other Indigenous peoples. It tricked people into debt, then forced them to work for no pay in harsh conditions.

Omarino's Witoto people lived in the Amazon rain forests of southeastern Colombia and northern Peru.

"We are sent far, far into the forest to get rubber. If we do not get it, or we do not get it quickly enough, we are shot."

Omarino

Brazilians working in conditions similar to those of slavery produce agricultural products such as sugar.

Modern Problem

Omarino and Ricudo eventually returned to South America. The enslavement of the Witoto only ended when the demand for rubber fell. Rubber companies decided to establish more **profitable** plantations in Southeast Asia.

Slavery remains a problem in the region, particularly in Brazil. Laborers from poor parts of the country are invited to work on ranches and plantations but are forced to work to pay the costs of moving to the job locations. They are paid far less than promised, so they cannot pay off their debt. Early in the 21st century, it was estimated that up to 40,000 people were working in Brazil in conditions of virtual enslavement.

Global Successes

The second half of the 19th and early 20th centuries brought successes for anti-slavery campaigners around the world.

Russia's system of **serfdom** dated from the mid-17th century. Serfs were tied to land, not owned by a person. Their lives were controlled by their landlord. Writer Alexander Radishchev wrote a book condemning serfdom in 1790. He was sent into **exile**. In 1825, Russian army officers staged a failed revolt against serfdom. In 1856, Czar Alexander II decided to abolish serfdom. The army was mainly made up of serfs, but they were poor soldiers so Alexander decided serfdom was not working. It was abolished in 1861.

Czar Alexander II finally abolished serfdom after the Russian army's poor performance in the Crimean War (1850–1853).

Slavery in the Congo

In West Africa, rubber companies enslaved people in the Congo Free State, a region owned privately by the Belgian king Leopold II. This continued even after a conference in Leopold's capital, Brussels, in 1890, agreed to end slavery. European missionaries revealed how Africans were forced to gather rubber by punishments such as having their limbs **amputated**. In 1908, the Belgian government took over control of the Congo from Leopold. Slavery was outlawed, although Africans there were still forced to gather rubber.

*From 1904, the British missionary Alice Seeley Harris photographed **mutilated** enslaved people in the Congo to support calls for abolition.*

Key Events

1890 Brussels Act

At a conference in Belgium, the leading Western nations committed themselves to the eradication of slavery around the world. The Brussels Act raised the profile of the anti-slavery campaign, although its plans contained no real strategies for ending slavery in places such as Africa.

Enslaved Women and Children

Although chattel slavery was outlawed by 1900, some forms of slavery remained common. The victims were often women and children.

Criminal gangs forced women into sex work, and used women and children for forced labor. In the 1910s, Rose Livingston campaigned to end the **sexual enslavement** of women in New York City. Rose had been kidnapped by criminals as a child and forced into sexual slavery. After she was rescued in the 1920s, she rescued young enslaved girls in Chinatown. She managed to save hundreds.

Schoolgirls in Nigeria hold signs in support of the kidnapped girls from Chibok, some of whom have been forced into slavery.

Key Events

Bring Back Our Girls Campaign

In April 2014, terrorists of the Boko Haram group took 276 teenage girls from a school in Chibok, Nigeria. The kidnapping was part of an ongoing struggle between Boko Haram and the Nigerian government. A campaign called Bring Back Our Girls was started to get the girls released. Some girls were rescued by the army and others were freed. However, in 2020, 112 girls were still missing. Many are feared to have been sold into slavery.

Kailash Satyarthi (right) won the Nobel Peace Prize in 2014, jointly with education activist Malala Yousafzai (left).

Saving the Children

The enslavement of women and children remains a problem in parts of Asia and Africa. Desperate families sometimes still sell their children into slavery to get money.

The campaigner Kailash Satyarthi worked as a teacher. In 1980, he gave up his job to protest child labor in his home country of India and elsewhere. He set up a team that rescued more than 88,000 child workers in India. In 1998, Satyarthi organized the first Global March against Child Labour. Activists protested in 103 countries. It eventually led to the International Labour Organization outlawing most forms of child slavery and labor.

CHAPTER 6

CAMPAIGNING AGAINST SLAVERY TODAY

After more than 200 years of activism, chattel slavery is now illegal everywhere. Other forms of slavery remain a problem around the world, however. Around 40 million people live in some form of slavery.

People are forced or tricked into working for little or no reward. They are controlled by threats of violence, punishment, or pay reduction. They sometimes have their passports taken away. Some are desperate people without money or education. Others are **migrants** with no legal status. The problem does not only affect developing countries. Slavery also appears in the United States, United Kingdom, and Canada.

French activists march to protest slavery in Libya. Activist organizations use such events to raise the profile of their causes. The sign reads, "I am human."

> Slavery is fundamentally illegal. Slavery happens because laws aren't being enforced.
>
> Nick Grono, human rights activist

Anti-Slavery International uses legal cases to test the laws against enslavement in countries where modern slavery exists.

Applying Pressure

According to the International Labour Organization, which is part of the United Nations, criminals earn $150 billion a year from illegal slavery.

The Anti-Slavery Society was founded in 1839 to campaign against chattel slavery. It took the lead campaigning against international slavery in the early 20th century. Later in the century, renamed Anti-Slavery International, it campaigned for legal changes to protect child laborers. It helped persuade the United Nations to appoint a Special Rapporteur on Contemporary Slavery in 2008. This led to greater investigation of slavery around the world. It also ensured that the focus was not just chattel slavery but also modern forms of slavery. The group also gives legal support to individuals in the hopes of creating legal **precedents** against slavery in specific countries.

Fighting Slavery

Mauritania, in northwest Africa, was the last country to ban slavery, in 1981. Slavery still exists in Mauritania, however, and laws against it have not been strictly applied.

The Mauritanian activist Biram Dah Abeid was born to enslaved parents. As a student, he founded the National African Movement to protest the enslavement of his Haratin ethnic group. He claimed that the whole state, including judges and the police, was resisting the abolition of slavery. In 2010, Biram Dah Abeid led a protest of about 80 supporters outside the home of a wealthy Mauritanian who owned two enslaved girls. The campaigners called for him to be arrested.

Biram Dah Abeid (right) is from the Haratin of Mauritania, who are descended from formerly enslaved people from southern Africa.

Key Voices

Temedt

The community group Temedt fights slavery in the African country of Mali. There, the Tuareg traditionally enslaved people. The practice continued after the abolition of slavery in the 1960s. Led by social leaders whose families have backgrounds in slavery, Temedt tries to change this view by challenging slavery through the courts.

It was only in 2007 that international pressure forced Mauritania to allow owners of enslaved people to be taken to court.

Eventually, the police did arrest him. This was the first time an owner of enslaved people had been arrested in Mauritania. However, Biram Dah Abeid was arrested, too. He spent more time in jail than the owner.

Prison Victory

Biram Dah Abeid continues to use his profile to call on the government to act against slavery. The government is reluctant to change. In 2018, it arrested him to prevent him from standing in elections, but he was elected as a Member of Parliament anyway. He argued that a **corrupt** president tolerated slavery because of racism toward the Haratin. He uses his position to insist that anti-slavery laws be enforced.

Human Trafficking

Modern slavery is often linked to human trafficking. Trafficking is the recruitment, harboring, or transportation of people for the purposes of forced labor or sexual exploitation.

Trafficking is often thought of as smuggling people from one country to another. Most often, however, it involves making people work for little money and with no choice. One leading anti-trafficking campaigner, Florrie R. Burke, became involved in 1997. She was asked to help provide social services to 60 deaf Mexicans. They had been enslaved in New York City and forced to beg to raise money for their employers.

Slavery is commonly seen as being mainly a problem of developing countries, but it happens everywhere.

Key Voices

The Freedom Fund

Human rights campaigner Nick Grono was a lawyer in Australia before becoming involved in the fight against slavery. He runs Freedom Fund, which raises money for programs to combat slavery and forced marriage. It has helped free more than 27,000 enslaved people and protect 400,000 poor people and women from exploitation.

A Continuing Struggle

Many organizations campaigning against modern slavery involve former victims of trafficking alongside other activists. The Polaris Project in the United States takes its name from the North Star that guided escaped enslaved people in the 1900s. Calls to its hotline have led to more than 50,000 people being rescued from slavery in the United States.

Halting human trafficking is difficult, however. It can be legally difficult to distinguish between slavery and what is simply low-paid work, which is not necessarily illegal. The arguments of activists against slavery will likely remain necessary for some time to come.

Protestors in London, England, get ready to take part in a "Walk for Freedom" march against modern slavery.

GET INVOLVED

Anyone can become an activist against modern slavery. Here are some suggestions of how to contribute.

1 Raise Funds

Groups fighting modern slavery rely on donations from supporters. Explore different organizations to find one whose methods you like, and check their website for ideas. Freedom United has a whole page of fundraising suggestions and stories: **www.freedomunited.org/fundraise**

2 Raise Awareness

You could help make sure as many people as possible are aware of the problem of modern slavery. The Polaris Project has infographics on human trafficking and the U.S. National Human Trafficking Hotline, specially designed to be shared over social media platforms: **https://bit.ly/39JaME9**

3 Volunteer

Anti-slavery organizations need volunteers to help with a range of activities from raising money to helping in the office. Look out for an organization near you that is in need of volunteers.

Stand Up!

Most organizations have an email list you can join for free. Sign up and stay in touch with what's happening in the fight against human trafficking. Check for anti-slavery events in your area. If there is a march, make a sign, tell others about the event, and show your support.

Stay Informed

It's important to educate yourself about the history of slavery around the world and stay up-to-date on modern slavery. Check your library for books about slavery and read about the subject on trusted websites, such as government sites or official organizations such as the United Nations.

Timeline

1518 The Spanish bring the first enslaved Africans to their Caribbean colonies.

1537 The Pope outlaws slavery in the Spanish Empire.

1619 The first enslaved Africans arrive in continental North America.

1688 Quakers in Germantown, Pennsylvania, write a *Petition Against Slavery*.

1775 Anthony Benezet founds the first anti-slavery organization in America.

1791 Olaudah Equiano writes the story of his life, the first in a series of narratives by enslaved people.

1831 Nat Turner launches a rebellion of enslaved people in Virginia, but it is put down by militia.

1833 Slavery is abolished in Great Britain.

1835 Enslaved African Muslims in Brazil begin the Malê Revolt.

1838 Frederick Douglass escapes from slavery. He becomes a leading activist against slavery.

1839 A group of Mende are freed by the U.S. Supreme Court after being illegally enslaved on the *Amistad*.

1849 Harriet Tubman escapes from slavery. She goes on to lead other enslaved people to freedom.

1859 John Brown's failed attempt to start a slave revolt ends in his execution.

1861 Serfdom is abolished in Russia.

1863 During the Civil War, Abraham Lincoln issues the Emancipation Proclamation.

1865 The Civil War ends, ending slavery in the United States.

1904 British missionaries use photography to campaign against slavery in the Belgian Congo.

1981 Mauritania becomes the last country in the world to ban slavery, although the ban is not supported by laws.

1998 Indian campaigner Kailash Satyarthi organizes the first Global March against Child Labour.

2008 Under pressure from groups such as Anti-Slavery International, the United Nations introduces a Special Rapporteur on Forms of Contemporary Slavery.

2014 The Bring Back Our Girls movement is founded to demand the release of hundreds of Nigerian schoolgirls, kidnapped by terrorists partly in order to sell them into slavery.

Sources

Chapter 1

"Brief History of Slavery." *New Internationalist*. August 2001. newint.org/features/2001/08/05/history

"What Is Modern Slavery?" Anti-Slavery International. www.antislavery.org/slavery-today/modern-slavery

Chapter 2

"The maroons of Jamaica." PortCities Bristol. www.discoveringbristol.org.uk/slavery/against-slavery/black-resistance-against-slavery/the-maroons-of-jamaica

Mueller, Anne Moore. "Early Protests." Quakers & Slavery. https://bit.ly/3ge373r

Tamari, Steve. "Haitian History as Antidote to Eurocentrism." Insidethemiddle. April 1, 2013. https://bit.ly/2D3hAAN

Chapter 3

"Olaudah Equiano." The Abolition Project. 2009. abolition.e2bn.org/people_25.html

Roxburgh, Ellis. *Nat Turner's Slave Rebellion* (Rebellions, Revolts, and Uprisings). New York: Gareth Stevens Publishing, 2017.

Chapter 4

Bordewich, Fergus M. "John Brown's Day of Reckoning." *Smithsonian Magazine*. October 2009. www.smithsonianmag.com/history/john-browns-day-of-reckoning-139165084

Gopnick, Adam. "The Prophetic Pragmatism of Frederick Douglass." *The New Yorker*. October 8, 2018. www.newyorker.com/magazine/2018/10/15/the-prophetic-pragmatism-of-frederick-douglass

Michals, Debra (Ed.) "Harriet Tubman." National Women's History Museum. 2015. www.womenshistory.org/education-resources/biographies/harriet-tubman

Chapter 5

"Forced labour in Brazil: 120 years after the abolition of slavery, the fight goes on." International Labour Organization. May 13, 2008. https://bit.ly/3ff1dxZ

Peck, Tom. "The mystery of the missing Amazonian rubber slaves." *The Independent*. August 2, 2011. https://bit.ly/3hSLKWk

Chapter 6

Hodal, Kate. "Mauritanian presidential hopeful arrested amid fears of political foul play." *The Guardian*. August 9, 2018. https://bit.ly/2EAQSzX

"Our History: Over 180 years of fighting slavery." Anti-Slavery International. https://bit.ly/2CWRzTQ

Glossary

abolition The act of officially ending or stopping something, such as slavery

abolitionists People who campaigned to end slavery

amputated Cut off

arsenal A place for storing weapons, ammunition, and military supplies

barbarian Describing a culture that is perceived to be uncivilized

bonded Employment agreement in which a person agrees to work to repay a debt, which is impossible to repay

chattel A personal possession

colonies Areas that are governed by a country in another part of the world

consent Agreement or permission

corrupt Acting dishonestly in return for money or personal gain

diplomat A government's official representative in another country

economically Related to money or trade

empires A large group of states or countries that are controlled by one ruler

exile The state of being banished from one's homeland

exploited Benefitted unfairly from someone's work

human rights Rights that belong to everyone, such as the right to live

human trafficking Buying or selling people illegally, or making money from work they are forced to do

indentured Bound by an agreement, or indenture, to work for someone for a set length of time, usually for little reward

Indigenous Describing the original inhabitants of a place

insurance Policies bought to protect a venture by providing payments in case of failure

Islamic Related to Islam, the religion of Muslims

Loyalists Americans who fought with the British during the American Revolution

martyr A person who is killed for their beliefs

Mennonite A follower of a strict form of Protestantism that started in Germany in the 1500s

migrants People who move to another country in search of better living conditions

militia A group of citizens trained to act as a military force in early colonies

missionaries People who promote a religion in another country

moral Concerned with the nature of right and wrong behavior

mutilated Badly and permanently injured

plantations Large farms for growing crops such as sugar, tobacco, or cotton

precedents Events such as legal cases that set a guide of what will happen in similar cases in the future

profitable Likely to make more money than what it cost to make a specific item

Quakers Members of a Christian group founded in England in the 1650s and dedicated to nonviolence

rebellion Resisting authority, control, or the way something is usually done

reform A change that improves a society or system

revolt A violent uprising against authority

serfdom The state by which peasants live on and are bound to specific piece of land and work for the person who owns the land

sexual enslavement Slavery in which women and girls are made to engage in sexual activity

tactics Methods for achieving goals

Further Information

Books

Behnke, Alison Marie. *Up for Sale: Human Trafficking and Modern Slavery*. Minneapolis: Twenty-First Century Books, 2014.

Paley, Caitlyn. *Slave Narratives and the Writings of Freedmen* (Primary Sources of the Abolitionist Movement). New York: Cavendish Square Publishing, 2015.

Roxburgh, Ellis. *The Amistad Revolt* (Rebellions, Revolts, and Uprisings). New York: Gareth Stevens Publishing, 2017.

Russo, Kristin J. *Viewpoints on the Underground Railroad* (Viewpoints and Perspectives). Ann Arbor, MI: Cherry Lake Publishing, 2018.

Sjonger, Rebecca. *What to the Slave Is the Fourth of July?* (Deconstructing Powerful Speeches). New York: Crabtree Publishing Company, 2020.

Stoltman, Joan. *Did the Abolition Movement Abolish Slavery?* (Key Questions in American History). New York: PowerKids Press, 2019.

Websites

autograph.org.uk/exhibitions/brutal-exposure-the-congo-international-slavery-museum
An online exhibition about slavery in the Congo, with interviews and a video.

www.thecanadianencyclopedia.ca/en/article/black-enslavement
A detailed account of the history of Black enslavement in Canada from *The Canadian Encyclopedia*.

www.history.com/topics/black-history/slavery
A history of slavery in the United States.

memory.loc.gov/ammem/aaohtml/exhibit/aopart3.html#03a
An online exhibit from the Library of Congress, with links to many primary sources about abolitionists and the abolition movement.

www.nationalgeographic.org/interactive/slavery-united-states
An interactive timeline of slavery in the United States from *National Geographic*.

www.unseenuk.org/modern-slavery/modern-slavery
A page from a British activist group explaining types of modern slavery, with links and videos.

Index